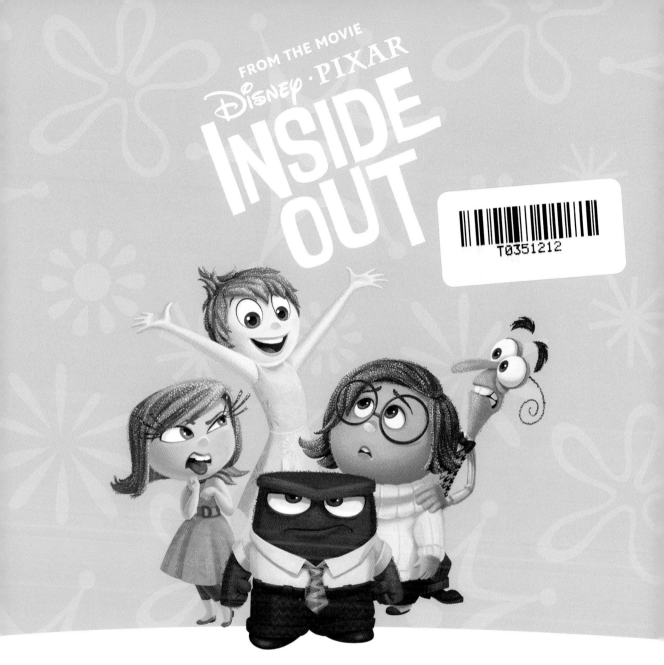

FROM THE MOVIE

Disney · PIXAR

INSIDE OUT

Level 4

Re-told by: Nicola Schofield
Series Editor: Rachel Wilson

Pearson Education Limited
KAO Two
KAO Park, Harlow,
Essex, CM17 9NA, England
and Associated Companies throughout the world.

ISBN: 978-1-2923-4683-0

This edition first published by Pearson Education Ltd 2020

7 9 10 8 6

Set in Heinemann Roman Special, 14pt/23pt
Printed by Neografia, Slovakia

Published by Pearson Education Limited

Acknowledgments
123RF.com: Dmitry Rukhlenko 24
Getty Images: Kristal O'Neal 24
Shutterstock.com: Blamb 26, decade3d - anatomy online 26,
Evgeny Bakharev 27, YummyBuum 24

For a complete list of the titles available in the Pearson English Readers series, visit
www.pearsonenglishreaders.com.

Alternatively, write to your local Pearson Education office or
to Pearson English Readers Marketing Department,
Pearson Education, KAO Two, KAO Park, Harlow, Essex, CM17 9NA

In This Book

Riley
A happy, 11-year-old girl who loves hockey

Joy
Riley's Emotion—she helps Riley to feel happy

Sadness
Riley's Emotion—she helps Riley to feel sad

Fear, Anger, and Disgust
Riley's other Emotions

Bing Bong
Riley's old friend who is part elephant, part cat, part dolphin

Headquarters
Riley's Emotions live here in Riley's mind

Before You Read

Introduction

Riley is a happy, 11-year-old girl. She lives in Minnesota with her parents. Riley's Emotions—Joy, Fear, Anger, Disgust, and Sadness live at Headquarters in Riley's mind. They help Riley every day and they want what is best for her. But when the family moves to San Francisco, there are big changes in Riley's life. Is it possible to stay happy?

Activities

1 **Read the sentences and say True or False.**

1 Riley is a young girl.
2 Riley lives with her friends.
3 Joy lives at Headquarters in Riley's house.
4 Riley's Emotions help her.

2 **Complete the sentences.**

unhappy   scared   happy   doesn't like many things   mad

1 Joy is …
2 Sadness is …
3 Fear is …
4 Anger is …
5 Disgust …

When Riley was born, Joy appeared. Then Disgust, Fear, Anger, and Sadness. They were Riley's Emotions. The Emotions worked together in Headquarters in Riley's mind and saw the world through her eyes.

Every day, they watched her eat, sleep, laugh, and play. The Emotions loved Riley. They always wanted to help her. This was easy when Riley was a baby.

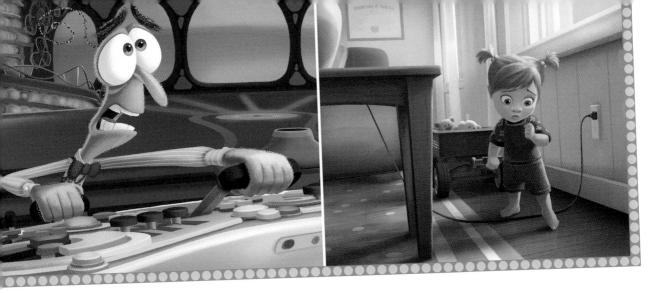

Fear was always scared. He watched Riley carefully and told her when it was dangerous. He didn't want her to fall or get hurt.

Anger was always angry. Sometimes Riley's parents cooked food that she didn't like. He didn't want Riley to eat it and he helped her to say no!

Disgust hated a lot of things. She helped Riley to choose what she didn't like. Vegetables were the worst—she hated them!
Sadness was always sad. She helped Riley when she felt unhappy.
One day, Riley's favorite toy broke. Riley cried!
Joy didn't want Riley to be sad. She wanted to keep Sadness away from Riley's memories.

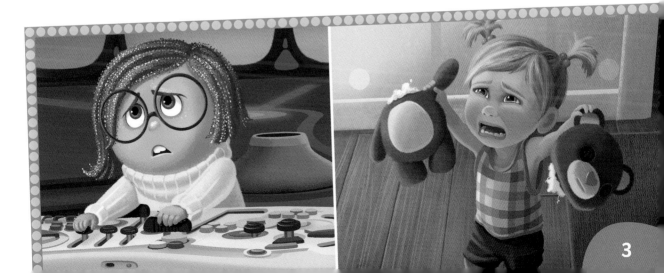

Headquarters was the most important place. All of Riley's special memories came here. When she was scared, the memories turned purple. When she was disgusted, they turned green. When she was angry, they turned red. When she was happy, they turned yellow, and when she was sad, they changed to blue. But Joy only wanted to keep yellow memories.

Outside Headquarters was Riley's Mind World. Riley's five Islands of Personality lived here—Family, Honesty, Hockey, Friendship, and Goofball.

Riley's five core memories controlled the islands. These were the most important memories of Riley's life and they sent power to the islands.

When Riley was little, there were many happy memories in Headquarters. This was Joy's plan and it worked.

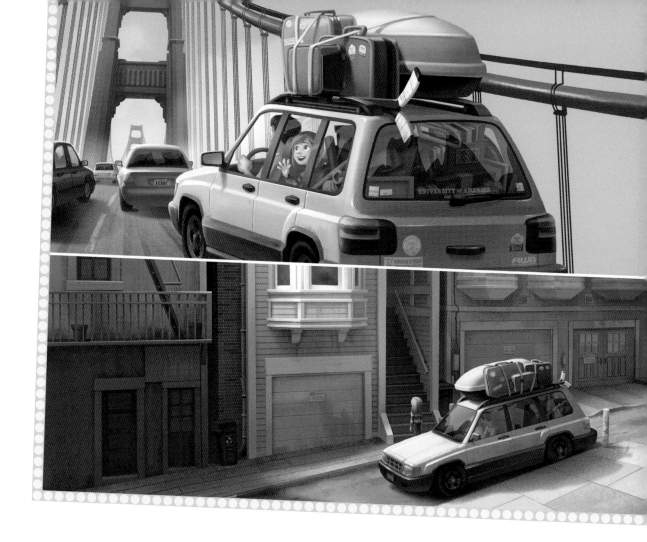

Then things changed … Riley's dad got a new job in San Francisco.
She was excited to move to a new city, live in a beautiful house,
and make new friends.

But when they arrived, the house was small and dark, and it
smelled funny.

In Headquarters, Joy tried to send Riley happy emotions.
She didn't want Riley to be sad.

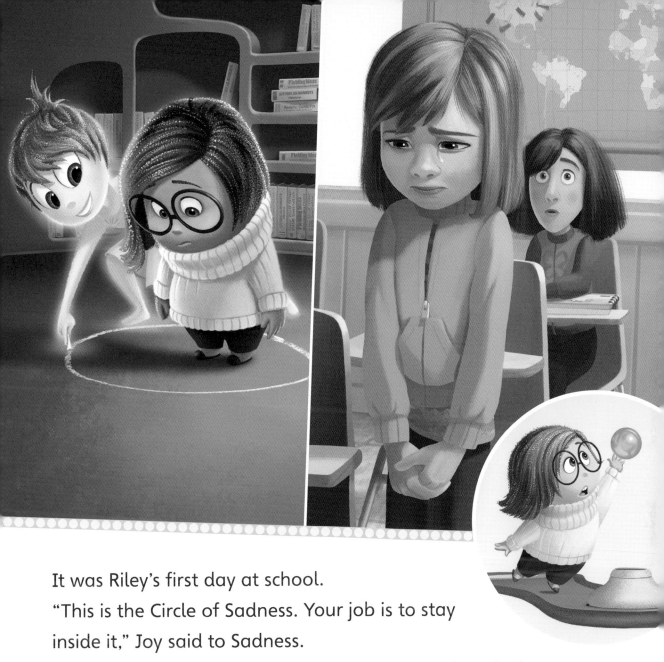

It was Riley's first day at school.

"This is the Circle of Sadness. Your job is to stay inside it," Joy said to Sadness.

The teacher asked Riley about Minnesota. Joy found a happy memory. "We go to the lake nearly every weekend," Riley said. Suddenly, Riley cried! For the first time, a blue core memory came into Headquarters.

There was panic in Headquarters! Joy jumped up quickly and tried to stop the sad memory.

Sadness tried to stop her, "Joy, no!"

CRASH! Riley's core memories fell on the floor. Then the lights from the five Personality Islands stopped working.

WHOOSH! Joy and Sadness didn't have any control. They flew out of Headquarters.

Joy and Sadness were now in Mind World. Joy quickly looked for Riley's five yellow core memories and carried them carefully. She couldn't find the blue memory.

Sadness was worried. How could Headquarters work without Joy? But Joy had some hope.

"We have to get back to Headquarters," she said. The nearest island was Goofball Island. They ran to it.

That night, Riley's parents asked her about her day at school.
Riley didn't want to talk about it.
Without Joy at Headquarters, it was difficult to control
Riley's emotions.
"No, no, no, stay happy!" shouted Fear.
Anger quickly took control and Riley shouted at her parents.
Riley's parents sent her to her room.

The islands started to fall fast. Goofball Island was the first.

"RUN!" shouted Joy.

They ran and arrived in Long Term Memory. Here, the memories that Riley could forget went to the Memory Dump. Then Friendship Island also started to fall. It was difficult to watch. The islands were part of Riley.

"Oh, Riley loved that one," said Sadness.

Suddenly, a friendly pink elephant appeared. Joy remembered
it was Bing Bong—Riley's old friend when she was three.
He was part elephant, part cat, and part dolphin!
He had so many happy and fun times with Riley. He loved Riley
very much. Joy really hoped that he could help.
Then, they lost Hockey Island …

Bing Bong had an idea. They could catch the Train of Thought to Headquarters. On the way to the station, Bing Bong saw his red rocket. It was an old memory with Riley and it was on its way to the Memory Dump.

"No, no, no. You can't take my rocket to the Memory Dump!" shouted Bing Bong.

Bing Bong started to cry.

"I know you and Riley had great times," Sadness said.

"They were wonderful," answered Bing Bong.

"Yeah, it's sad," said Sadness.

Joy watched Sadness and saw how she helped Bing Bong to feel better.

"I'm okay now," he said. "Come on, the train station is this way."

Joy started to understand that it was okay to feel sad.

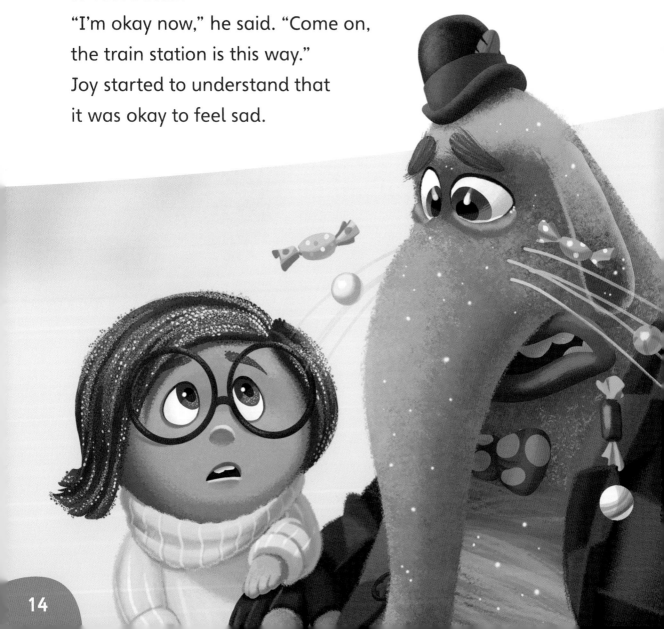

They arrived at the station. On the train, Joy and Sadness talked about their favorite memory—one of Riley's hockey games. Sadness only remembered that Riley lost the game— all the sad parts of the memory. Joy wanted to help Sadness remember the happy parts. Suddenly, Honesty Island started to fall and the train quickly stopped.

Family Island began to fall and Long Term Memory broke
open. A tube appeared that took memories to Headquarters.
"We can use the tube!" cried Sadness.

But Joy didn't want Sadness to turn the core memories blue,
so she jumped into the tube without Sadness. The tube broke
and Joy, and all the core memories, fell out!

Bing Bong tried to catch Joy but the ground fell below him.
He and Joy fell into the Memory Dump.
In the Dump, Joy found the memory of the hockey game.
She remembered how Riley's parents and friends made Riley
feel happier after the game. She understood that the happy
part of the memory only happened because Riley felt sad.

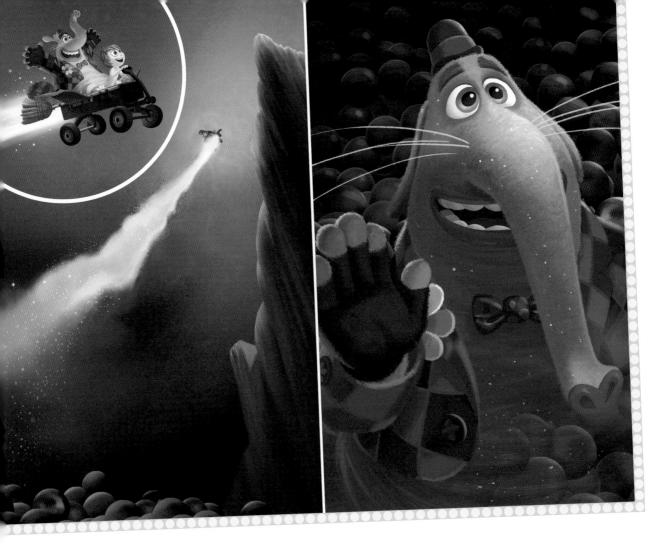

Suddenly, Joy had an idea. They could ride Bing Bong's
rocket out of the Memory Dump! They found the rocket and
hopped in. They sang their loudest and the rocket flew up!
But it was small and Bing Bong was heavy. He jumped out
and stayed behind.

"Woo-hoo! Bing Bong, we did it!" cried Joy.

"You made it! Go save Riley!" he shouted.

Joy saw Sadness crying on a cloud. She jumped off Family Island, caught Sadness, and they flew to Headquarters. They made it back!

"Sadness, it's your turn," said Joy.

She gave Sadness the five core memories and Riley began to cry. She told her parents that she was sad. Riley felt better quickly and the memories became blue and yellow.

Riley's life soon became easier. She made new friends, played hockey, and was happy in San Francisco. At Headquarters, Joy and Sadness were also happy. Joy understood that it's okay to be sad sometimes. Sadness tried to see the good things in unhappy times. They understood that the best way to help Riley was to work together.

After You Read

1 **Finish the sentences.**

1 In Minnesota, Riley is …

   a happy   **b** scared   **c** sad

2 Joy thinks that Riley can …

   a win hockey games   **b** be happy all the time   **c** run fast

3 At first, Riley's life in San Francisco is …

   a easy   **b** difficult   **c** good

4 Bing Bong is a friend …

   a from hockey   **b** from Riley's school   **c** from Riley's mind

2 **Who says this?**

> Joy   Riley   Sadness   Bing Bong   Fear

1 "We go to the lake nearly every weekend."
2 "I know you and Riley had great times."
3 "Your job is to stay inside it."
4 "No, no, no, stay happy!"
5 "You can't take my rocket to the Memory Dump!"

3 **Discuss the questions with a friend.**

1 Why does Riley cry in school?
2 Why is Bing Bong sad when he sees his rocket?

Glossary

appear past tense **appeared** (*verb*) to suddenly be there; *When Riley was born, Joy appeared.*

control past tense **controlled** (*verb*) to have the power to make a person or thing do what you want; *Joy and Sadness didn't have any control.*

core (*adj.*) the most important; the center; *Riley's five core memories controlled the islands.*

disgusted (*adj.*) when you really don't like something; *When she was disgusted, her memories turned green.*

dolphin (*noun*) a large, gray, intelligent animal that lives in the ocean

emotion (*noun*) a feeling; *happiness and sadness are emotions.*

hurt (*adj.*) when you fall, you can hurt your body; *He didn't want her to fall or get hurt.*

mad (*adj.*) very angry; *We have to go home before I REALLY get mad!*

memory (*noun*) when you remember a thing, person, or place from the past

mind (*noun*) a part of the body that helps you think and feel

panic (*noun*) when you are suddenly very scared and you don't know what to do

save past tense **saved** (*verb*) to stop a person from getting hurt or dying; *Go save Riley!*

together (*adj.*) with one or more people; *They understood that the best way to help Riley was to work together.*

tube (*noun*) a long, thin, round thing that a person or a thing can go through

unhappy (*adj.*) not happy; *Sadness tried to see the good things in unhappy times.*

worried (*adj.*) you feel worried when you have a problem or when you don't know about the future; *Sadness was worried. How could Headquarters work without Joy?*

Phonics

Say the sounds. Read the words.

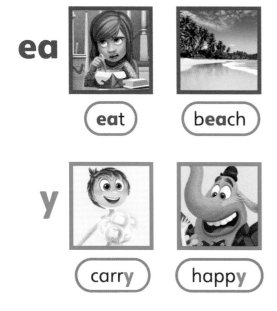

ea (eat) (beach)   ee (green) (sleep)

y (carry) (happy)

Say the poem.

Riley's life is happy.
Suddenly, one weekend,
She leaves for a new city,
And she can't see her friends.
Is she sleeping or dreaming?
How does the story end?

Values

Talk about your feelings.

25

Emotions—what is happening inside your brain?

There is a part of your brain—deep in the core—called the **amygdala** (am-ig-da-la). It *controls* your emotions of anger and fear. It helps you to move quickly without thinking—to run away or to fight when there is danger. This could save your life! But it could also make you panic and stop thinking. The **frontal lobe** is also part of the brain. It helps *you* to control your emotions of anger and fear. It helps *you* to think and plan what to do.

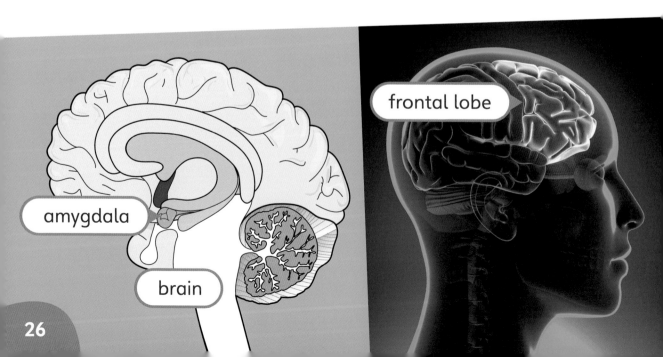

amygdala

brain

frontal lobe

How can you control your emotions?

Breathing deeply helps to control anger and fear. It helps you to use your frontal lobe and *think*!

Try this:

- close your eyes
- breathe deeply five times
- think of a beautiful, yellow flower
- in your mind, smell and touch it
- breathe deeply five more times
- open your eyes

How do you feel?

danger (*noun*) you're in danger when a thing that is happening—or you're doing—is dangerous
breathe (*verb*) to take air into your body through your nose or mouth